# DATE DUE

# HOLD APRIL

# HOLD APRIL

New Poems by Jesse Stuart

Woodcuts by Walter Ferro

McGraw-Hill Book Company, Inc.
New York    Toronto    London

A listing of previously copyrighted
material will be found on page 112.

*For Jane*

Hold on to April; never let her pass!

Another year before she comes again

To bring us wind as clean as polished glass

And apple blossoms in soft, silver rain.

# Contents

# Love song after forty

## I

Knee-deep in leaves, in milkweed furze with
    sawbrier trimming,
Your hand mine holds, your willowy body leaning
So your autumn-colored, curly hair is against my face
    and shoulder:
So deep in love, in autumn's splendor lucently dying,
So late in love our autumn is almost over,
Again we softly kiss, unmindful our time is inexorably going
To a secret place that is not beyond our knowing.
While time is left, let us pretend we are not caring
How little remains. We keep on living, loving, daring.

### II.

Come, put your shoulder
In the curve of my arm
Before we are older,
And time is colder,
Be all you are to me.

As under old leaves
Where lost youth repines,
Where late wind grieves,
For love's old reprieves,
The late sun shines.

Higher and higher
Where the dim path goes,
By a late primrose.
There is more to admire
Where the late leaf goes.

III.

Burnt-orange maple leaves drift indolently down,
Burgundy-wine chestnutoak leaves,
Buff-colored hickory leaves,
Tangerine-red sumac,
Apple-red persimmon,
Pumpkin-yellow sugartree,
Cockscomb-red maple,
All rain their mixture to the ground.
We like the wind and leaf-rain sound.

Foxtail gray,
Ripe-cornstalk brown,
Sumac-berry red,
Turkey-wattles red,
Pumpkin yellow,
Maroon,
Multicolored drops zigzag down
From the colored rain-clouds to the ground.

Poplar leaves are the color of the bright full moon
On a winter night or an evening in June,

But the sere ash leaves are as gray-bellied
As a butterfly's winter-wan cocoon.

IV.

The second ledge has views that are sublime—
Where drowsier mumbling bumblebees
Put their last accents on the wasting flowers,
Where a mountain daisy blooms beneath the thyme,
Until plucked by this hand to fasten in your hair.
Pairs of barking squirrels play through the somber trees,
And pairs of birds, each to their kind, sing in the bowers,
Sing on their flights together through the air,

                                        Sing everywhere!
On this high level there is no despair.

V.

Unbored,
We have soared
On levels where life's patterns run—
Springtime with blossoms in our eyes,
With the bright wings of butterflies,
And summertime with growth and sun,
A time to shape and mould the things undone.
Unbored, we have soared,
Until older, yes, but none too wise,
For we have starlight in our eyes.

## VI

Unafraid,
We have made
Over half the circle of the clock
Ignoring its persistent tick-tock.
Enthusiastic, with time left to take
Love's elevator higher than the sun,
Since love is not measured by the sky,
But by the acts and deeds we have done.
Love is not measured by verse meter,
Nor by the wind,
Nor by the bees' last accents on the flowers.
True love cannot be bought and sold,
For it is all that it implies:
Substantial, and as certain as stars in the skies.
For many, true love is difficult to find,
And, for a few, impossible to hold
To engrave upon the heart and mind,
Since an ounce of it cannot be bought
With an acorn cup of fairy gold.

# The day I drove my truck

Out of the wintry past I still remember
The day I drove my truck into the wood
In filagreed, clean frost of late November,
I saw a thing that almost chilled my blood.
Turning a log embedded in the ground
Where there was roof and wall against the cold,
My setter's sniffling so quickly found
A pretty, parent, baby-handed mole.
There in her nest he crushed her instantly,
But not the babies suckling at her breast,
Whose small eyes were still closed in infancy
And bodies were exposed to winter's blast.
This scene remains embedded in my brain:
I took four naked young from their dead mother
Into my home against the sleet and rain
And raised them on goat's milk with an eye-dropper.

# Song

Hard knuckles of the wind knock on my door.
The clock strikes twelve.

                          Another year has ended.

I stop my work with papers on the floor
And put away the books that have befriended
Me on so many nights before the fire.
Time at my heels has never brought me fears.
Someday Time will catch me.

                              I shall retire

Since mortal flesh cannot outlast the years.
Time cannot make me tremble like the leaf!
I look into the empty night and stare,
Midnight is lonely and is filled with grief;
Out there tonight is the ghost of yesteryear.
High in the midnight sky the bright stars glisten
While I begin my New Year with a song—
A melody to make the people listen.
I'll sing for all—the poor, the weak, the strong!

# Why ever grieve

Why ever grieve for blighted bloom and leaf
When Winter fought the Spring to keep his crown;
His second coming was a time so brief,
But long enough to sow his death-seeds down.
Why ever grieve for all this bitter strife
Since Spring returns with certainty and pride
To frozen Earth with promise of new life
With Nature her assistant and her guide.
The flowers that Winter killed will grow again
And cloaks of green adorn each naked tree
With Nature's healing sun and soothing rain.
With wordless blueprints from eternity
Nature will reproduce the broken parts,
Make flowers grow from old roots in the sod
When we can't grow new arms and make new hearts,
Don't question man but ask Almighty God.

# Time passes

An empty house can soon deteriorate
And birds take over eave and chimney stone,
And hinges red with rust on door and gate
Are signs to show that time has come and gone.
The golden wasps will find a way to enter
After one pulls the shades and bolts the door
To gallivant and die in cool midwinter
On windowpanes, in beds and on the floor.
The flimsy furtive moth will not be kind
To take the best one has to suit his taste;
The mice will enter, multiply and find
Books, manuscripts and everything to waste.
The sturdy walls one builds cannot shut out
Collective dampness and night-colored gloom
Where uninvited guests have brought about
Destruction to each nicely furnished room.

# Pockets

This time is running out for each of us
Who walks a mortal's rugged road but once,
While speechless summer leaves hang tremulous
And silent are the strata of old stone.

In man's sojourn he questions why and if
He is the individual son of God,
Why he is parted by the wall and cliff,
Indifferent clime and worn impoverished sod.

Beauty there is and purity in him
Who clings to life upon this battered ball,
Brutality, inconsequential dream
If each could see behind the other wall!

Time is as endless as a man is frail
And multicolored images who seek
Security on earth to no avail
Are pockets paying for their being weak.

Real or imaginary wall, thin sod,
Knowledge and beauty will soon penetrate
And men world-over will be sons of God,
And what are pockets now, be obsolete.

# Autumn poem

Lately, he has seen autumn in her cheek
Nearly so beautiful as once the rose;
This hurts him deeply and he does not speak,
Thinking she'll go the way the blossom goes.
He wonders why the rose too soon must die,
A flower most beautiful the soonest goes,
No longer pointing blossoms to the sky,
To kiss with honey-fragrance wind that blows.
For her he thinks late autumn will come soon
Since in her cheeks the colors cease to thrive,
Colorless bloom beneath cool autumn's moon,
And he must be the stubborn oak alive.
He knows the autumn oak protects the rose,
The flower most beautiful, the soonest goes.

# Schoolmaster, once

It is most painful now as I
Schoolmaster once return to this;
Master of learning, all they had
Until they grew and went beyond.
This barn was dear to them and me.
Only the skeleton remains;
Parts of the roof, windows and doors
And master's desk and window panes
Are gone into oblivion.

The birds and bats now carry on,
Where elm trees have reached new heights;
Young winds blow over greened-up fields
That lie in all directions here
Where fields of grass run with the winds.
These friendly winds have not erased
The memories of what has been
From those who caught fire here that spread
The flame of learning to the world.

# Man and his valley

Valley with lyric voice in winter wind,
What lies beyond your depths of stirring sound?
Trees are etched on soft evening's blue blind,
Old restive leaves are wood nymphs on the ground.
I am man's living symbol of your clay
And cool dirt words you speak are not in vain.
I thirst for you when I have gone away;
Tonight I drink,
     But I shall thirst again.
My valley of the close eternal tie,
When you are gay,
     I am filled with delight.
And when you grieve and autumn night winds cry,
I walk enthralled into your starry night.
What lies hidden
     I do not understand
Infinite wisdom of this workable plan
That everything is oneness with the land,
When you are valley and I am the land.

# Summer writes another book

Each specie of the migratory bird
Is now assembling with its flock,
And mumbling honeybees detained by chilly winds
Find little nectar in the autumn flowers.
The hungry, thin-winged butterflies grow numb
And fall down steps of wind in search of flowers.
Slow, dwindling streams sing drowsily
Beneath soft trickling of untimely leaves.
These are the closing pages of a book.

Queen-of-the-Meadow blossoms rejoice
Nodding in all directions to the drowsy winds
And yellow leaves drip to the ground
Beneath vine-tangles rich with harvest.
Lazy terrapins roll down the bluffs
And crawl across the dusty road
And narrow bottoms to the brackish streams
Where they shall quench their thirst
And find a place to hibernate.
Reddening of sumac berries
On leafless antlers in the wind
Is an exciting paragraph.

All living things that fly, walk, run and crawl
Can read this book in their own language.
Summer is a linguist who writes in many tongues.

The goldenrod that's everywhere,
Blue and white farewell-to-summer on the slopes
And multicolored morning-glory bells that glow
From vines entwining stalks of ripened corn
Is lyric poetry in this book.
Each row of knee-high stubble in the field
Where corn is cut in wigwam foddershocks,
Each thumb-high stubble where cane and tobacco grew
And close-shorn, flimsy stubbles of the wheat
Are strong, substantial sentences.

This book, Nature has just released
Is powerful from beginning to end.
Each sentence, paragraph, and page, will hold one
Reading new winds as fuzzy as an August peach.
The structural sentences in the sky
And on the lonesome leaf, both new and different,
Make transitional paragraphs between
The stone, tree, valley, landscape and cloudscape.
Everything that flies, runs, walks, and crawls
Will depend upon the reader's interpretation.

# Green river

Green winter river flowing to the sea
Between snow-covered banks and barren trees,
I speak to you and you speak back to me
With interruptions of a winter breeze.
In seasons past my love and I have stood
Beneath your willow, elm and sycamore
And hummed tunes to the music of your flood,
And written lyrics to your lilting roar.
We do not always sing and make a rhyme
In spring beneath your fluffy, green-cloud shade;
We go to you in leaf and blossom time
And in the hours with you our dreams are made.
Flow on, take to warm seas your winter ice
Down rippling green between white strips of foam,
But, bring spring back, days balmy warm and nice;
We'll make your winding course our springtime home.

# Land where the honey-colored wind is fair

Give them leaf-laundered wind to breathe again,
Land where the honey-colored wind is fair,
Fondling the yellow stems of dying grain,
Combing the broomsedge fields long, golden hair.
Give them a land of melancholy wind
To stir music in them eternally;
They would want sight if they were going blind,
And if tone-deaf, they would like melody.
They have breathed carbon on too many roads
And choking smoke in cities near and far;
They have been too submissive to strange fads,
Now let them wear the wind and sun and star.
The lonesome water's wordless, soothing songs
Are great for them beneath their bluer skies;
Nature's mistakes are better than man's wrongs,
Give them love language of the wild birds' cries.

# Impressions

Often our lives mirrored in troubled waters,
We were the victims of most unfortunate moods:
Sensational morning news made our heads ache,
Coffee and nicotine then stimulated
Our aching heads, TV's blazed all the day,
Papers bearing banner headlines were filled
With killings, rapes, teens, more A and H
Bombs.
　　　　　Why had we left the farms for urbias?
Where was the time and place for us to think?
We smoked, drank coffee, ate our aspirins,
Took happy pills to sooth our jangled nerves—
Tranquilizer was the technical name.

Our 1957 summer drought
Upset our temperaments.
　　　　　　　　Thirty-five days
Without one lucid drop to moisten air!
We took more aspirins, tranquilizers,
Inhaled more nicotine, drank blacker coffee
Beneath parched skies, breathed brittle wind—
Brittle, bone-dry, unlaundered, raspy wind.
We were unfriendly with each other; then,
A shower came to wet the lips of earth,

And thirsty, juiceless plants looked up and smiled
And we rejoiced: forgetting aspirins,
Coffee, nicotine, and tranquilizers:
We drove our power-laden autos through
The shower: Three hundred h.p. more or less,
Half-century advanced beyond our roads,
Our county's capital receiving us
In clouds of steam that rose from heated streets
Rain-cooled; we parked our cars with sharkfin lines
That split the burning wind at ninety miles:
Three hundred h.p. unleashed on high octane!
We walk in rain on unsufficient legs;
We talk to neighbors we've not seen in years;
Come often rain to give us friendly mood.
Come often rain to save our pocketbooks.
You make us take vacation time with friends;
Make us unbend, relax; you make us laugh;
You make us leave our individual cells!
You make; you make; you make; Come often rain!
Descending on our county capital
Which is no longer center of our world:
With cars America is our domain.
This little rain has hurt our drugstore sales;
For years there has not been a time like this
When laughter fills the air and water fills
The streets. We know each other better now.
This rain is better than millions that we spend
On social, get-together, propaganda.
Nature. You make; you make; Come often rain!

# Spring voices

This is not the wind in the weeping willow tree
Who speaks to me on a convalescing bed
Placed by the window where I hear and see,
These are real voices, not dreams in my head!
They have returned, these lovers long departed
To this fair valley where they used to be;
They come unseen when the spring blooms have started
To talk, laugh, sing and love as merrily
As pairs of singing bluebirds in the spring
Who have their nests with eggs in tree and post;
With April songs they make this valley ring,
Of all our songbirds, bluebirds sing the most.
Their singing vies with lovers I can't see
Who talk and laugh beneath the willow tree.

# The two houses

The house I chose to build has many doors
From room to room and through the outer wall,
And I have rugs and carpets on the floors
To muffle noise time makes with each footfall.
I built in freedom but well-disciplined
My own small house to stand awhile in space,
To comfort me against time, thirst, and wind,
To have some pets and flowers around my place.
I made this house with many windows too,
I could not have too many panes for light
In windows of my walls where I could view
Through their transparency the velvet night.
Someday, I'll have a house not of my choice
Without a pane betwixt me and the day,
No music, mirth, not one familiar voice
Or door or window in its walls of clay.

# Heart-summoned

Sometimes in bonnet that she used to wear
And faded dress by wild-rose brambles torn,
She moves so lightly on her path of air
As she returns, a mother to her son.
She does not knock nor does she come within
To tell me who her new companions are:
She vanishes upon her path of wind,
Accompanied, perhaps, by cloud or star.

# Extended invitation

I knew this Master Host would hold me in
His clayey house where millions now reside,
Where there would be no folded hills, no wind,
No way of knowing whom I slept beside.

The branches on his trees would be austere
Without a blossom or an April spring.
Being his guest how could I rise to hear
From my dark lonely room just one bird sing?

A candidate who met him face to face
And though selected as a single choice
Did not want him to take me from life's race,
Tether my fleeting feet or still my voice.

# Autumn sequence

### I.

There is no need for one to say the bee
Has come to gather honey from the clover
And honeydew from leaves of sweetgum tree,
It is too late because the summer's over
With frosted petals of late flowers dying.
And strange winds whining in the tangled grass.
High overhead the southbound geese are flying
Up in bright wind clean as polished glass;
Only what is to die is dead or dying,
What once was flowering is now decay.
The bees and butterflies have stopped their flying.
Their wings returned to dust winds blew away.
This wind tells one while kissing his cool face,
Summer at last has finished its short race.

### II.

Her heart beats faster when she thinks of leaves
That color under autumn's copper sun;
When she hears in the trees a wind that grieves
She feels her long life's course is nearly run.
Leaves that are severed from wind-harried tree
She feels the blood of these under her sky
Is substance of the blood that flows in her;
Leaves blown by wind to fields where they must lie

Beneath the facts of time and wind and star.
These are the facts that never know decay.
Why can't she be as changeless as these are?
Why must she follow in a seasonal way?
Why must she be as leaves that leave no trace
Where she began or left life's little race?


### III.

Never was night as wind-swept beautiful!
Blow by them winds, in deep poetic mood!
Go whine among the sedge where cidia lull,
But do not chill poor circulating blood.
Never were they as humble as tonight
To see the beauty they can never own
From hours of darkness to the hours of light,
From shining star to petal, leaf, and stone.
Winds whisper they are dreamers in this world
Who soon must lie asleep until the spring
When resurrected life will be unfurled,
Leaf, bloom, and seed and hibernating thing!
Winds tell them to enjoy autumn if they must
Since earth must soon collect its rented dust.


### IV.

Approaching chill of autumn makes blood run
As slow through vein as sap in ancient tree;
When it was young and warmed by April sun

It raced up veins of sapling sunwardly.
Approaching autumn wind makes lizards stir
And sleepy snakes seek hibernating hole,
And drowsy scorpions search for sun somewhere
And dizzy wasp return to oaken bole.
Demented autumn wind that lifts the leaf
Weeps hypocritically and weeps alone
For all of those whose lifetimes were too brief,
Weeps for their flowers too whose blooms are gone.
Demented autumn wind is lonely here,
Weeping above an earth that is their bier.


v.

Autumn is not forever for the land,
It brings new beauty and a change of season;
Life in declension follows death's command,
Then sleeps and knows rebirth for valid reason.
Life is linked with the Sun from birth to death.
O, mighty Sun! Let us now thank the Sun!
Be grateful for life under its warm sheath
That shines on us until our lives are done.
*O, mighty Sun, above our ancient gods!*
*O, mighty Sun, above our autumn earth!*
*O, Sun, without you we could have no foods!*
*You nurture plants from birth until their death.*
*Our gift, O, mighty Sun, are plants from you!*
*We lift, O, mighty Sun, a chant to you!*

40

Play lively mighty autumn violins
Dance tunes upon this earth's uneven floor;
Play swiftly in the briers where old snake skins
Will fool the flocks of hungry crows no more.
Blast forth you mournful trumpets of late thunder!
Swish down, you dismal drumming of the rain!
This is the time to put the old life under;
Let it be resurrected life again!
Play for this season's passing from the earth!
Play for man, salamander, snake, and newt!
Play for the crickets on the farmer's hearth!
Play for the seeds of life to sprout and shoot!
Play lullabies for those who are asleep,
Drown with your lively tunes all those who weep!

# This is the place

This is the place that time has long forgot
Where sawbriers mingle with wild rose and thorn
High on this ridge, this lone deserted spot
Where men have lived and died where they were born.
No one knows now their little dream and trust,
Their hunger, thirst, desire, toil, love and hate
That have evaporated with their dust.
High-moaning, mountain winds cannot relate
The lives they lived on this steep, rugged ground;
Tall trees on land they farmed now have grown here
And bend to these high winds in plaintive sound.
The sleeping sprouts and briers are leafless, sear,
In this hay-yellow light of winter sun;
The perky redbird sings a note of cheer
For life that has been here and lost and won
Where wild rose, sawbriers, and tall trees appear.

# Songs that sing themselves

Bright July is a month when warm winds rove
Over the green-cloud hills and through the wheat,
Up valleys, through lace fern and bracken cove,
Each puff a sonnet I cannot repeat.
The hungry bees like fields of Queen Anne's lace
And butterflies feast on the dusty yarrow;
Their bright wings flash through lazy, sunlit space,
What will they do, where will they go tomorrow?
Each lonely day she spends is a fickle coin
While stalwart corn turns golden in the furrow.
All fragile life will know when summer's gone
Into bright fields of autumn death and sorrow.
And we who hear these July songs rejoice,
Though poignant lyrics often bring a tear;
The songs that sing themselves have been my choice,
Now we must wait until another year.

# Come gentle snow

Move closer, faster, storm clouds over earth,
Enfold it in a blanket clean and white;
This time of thaw earth's floor is soft beneath
Our feet and scars unpleasant to our sight.
For many months our Mother Earth has lain
Under white sheet, beneath a weaker sun,
Until warm winds blew in and brought us rain.
Now streams down small ravines to valleys run.
In littered yards no tin cans take the eye,
Protective cover does no longer hide
The naked earth under a high blue sky.
Unlike some folks, the snow and grass have pride.
Come gentle snow before the winter's over,
Too long away are legions of the grass.
Spread over earth your clean and wholesome cover
To hide with loveliness these scars we pass.

# Shelter

Thin, racing, rain-clouds came down from the North
So low they touched the earth's green thirsting breast;
Ahead of them two silent crows winged South
Toward a pine grove and their hidden nest.

Approaching clouds, the color of cane-juice,
Fetched winds that made the cornblades tremble some;
And beech limbs in the valley swinging loose
Were whispering that rain had finally come.

Then, everywhere about, each greening shoot
Turned its leaflips in prayer toward the skies;
A kildee family rose in wild dispute,
Climbing the stairs of wind with startling cries.

My mule and I ran for a rockcliff roof
And got there dripping wet like arms of trees;
Thankful, we rested in a room rain-proof
And through wind-windows watched rejoicing leaves.

Deep in the white slabs of the welcomed rain
We watched our thirsting corn drink with a will;
We watched stalks bow in thanks and rise again—
Corn drinking rain is something beautiful!

We rested patiently in our dry room
Away from storm and wet wind-touseled weeds;
We smelled clean fragrance of wild phlox in bloom
And watched the lace ferns' dripping silver beads.

My mule with sparkling eyes and tight-drawn lips
Shook raindrops from his ears and close cropped mane
While he dreamed of the rain-washed clover-tips
And tender sweetblades of the growing cane.

My dreams were for the future, I could see
My autumn cornfields with the stubble dead;
I could not let the winter come on me,
Without corn for my cattle and my bread.

I dreamed of corn enough to fill my bin,
Straight rows of perfect grains so smooth and white,
Of summer's ending, winter's setting in,
Of frozen fields frost-glistening in moonlight.

I could not live through summer helter-skelter
And like the grasshopper beg winter bread;
My bin must be security's safe shelter
When all my fertile fields are winter-dead.

# The wind's triumphant note

Wind in the trees sounds out a triumphant note
Down lost green avenues of timbered slope
At midnight when the silvery moon's afloat
And lengthening shadows crane long necks and grope.
Wind has played dirges winter-long for us
Like cold rain beating tom-toms on the cliffs;
Now it can sing a victory song for us
Since leaf and bloom hide winter's hieroglyphs.
Moon-glistening tassels on the healthy corn
Are fair incentive, stimulating power,
While sweet hilarious fragrance of the morn
Awakes each dewy blade and cornsilk flower.
Wind sings for us each day along our march
In ripen'd blades and over golden mound;
The rainbow forms a many-colored arch
Through which we pass over productive ground.

# A sincere song

Each morn I rise before my world awakes
To breathe sweet winds of morning from wild flowers;
I like soft sounds the early morning makes
While earth is sleeping in her twilight hours.
I like the sincere songs of rising birds
Who put new life into beginning day;
Birds' songs are better than a poet's words
In mild midsummer's early roundelay.
Softly I walk upon my waking world
Where lesser lyric streamlets speak to me,
Where brown-eyed Susans' petals are dew-curled,
Their dark eyes winking at eternity.
A few midsummers more the birds will miss
My searching when the morning winds have died;
Ghost-figure in the quiet haziness,
Searching for something, never satisfied.

# Sandy will flow forever

Sandy will flow forever to the sea
Beneath the clouds of green leaves on the willows;
Sandy will flow as long as winds are free
And ironweeds purple on the summer meadows.
Now I shall catch a breath of wind tonight,
Walk down this twisted road beneath the moon;
And I will surely find one song to write
Where whippoorwills and cornfield insects croon.
And Sandy River mad with April showers
Flows headlong down spring's corridors of green,
Her grassy banks whitewashed with April flowers
As pretty as this mortal eye has seen.

# Unforgotten

What are the dreams within his white old head
As he totters down the street, tapping his cane
Where leaves are drifting golden, yellow, red?
Does he dream of a long forgotten spring?

He must dream of a honeymoon long past,
Of her—red-lipped, blue-eyed with auburn hair.
He wonders why their springtime could not last
And why she had to go who was so fair.

Gone is her song and laughter he has known,
Her touch of hand and softly spoken word,
Each one a yellow leaf in the wind's wild moan.
Another spring returns now, he has heard,

The sweetest sounds this side of paradise
Within the confines of his little world;
He stumbles on, for warm tears blind his eyes—
A lonely autumn leaf, gently wind-swirled.

# Once on a solitary walk

Once on a solitary walk I found
Deep in an autumn wood where sassafras
And sawbrier leaves were knee-deep on the ground
A small peach growing in this wilderness,

And there upon the topmost fragile shoot
Three peaches bent the little branch with weight
And I reached down and plucked this bright-red fruit
And stood amid this wilderness and ate

The most delicious fruit I ever knew,
The sweet lush flesh of red October cling,
Such fruit from this small seedling tree that grew
From earth so poor it scarce could grow a thing

Where sassafras, sawbrier and sumac thrived.
This fruit tree never had a guiding hand,
Smothered in sterile soil, yet it survived,
A good seed dropped upon a fruitless land.

# The snow lies patched

The snow lies patched on our enduring hills
Where surfaces first face the morning sun;
Snow-water mumbles down slow winter rills
But stops when sunset freezing has begun.
And winter birds seek shelter for the night
In fodder shocks and in the frozen grass
And shadows of owls' wings in pale moonlight

Frighten the timid rabbits when they pass.
And then to see an evening silhouette
Of snow-patched crazy quilt against the moon,
Enduring beauty one cannot forget
That cannot come too often or too soon.
On cone-shaped northside slopes the snow lies deep
Where weakened winter suns can't penetrate
And barren oaks wind-creak in frozen sleep
Unmindful night is long when spring is late.

# Dawn

### I.

Before dawn I stood on this eternal hill—
Rockbed of my foundation,
Waiting for my autumn world to wake;
Watching him rub sleep from his eyes
With rockcliff knuckles,
Mountain range arm
Broad, calloused, plateau hand
Which fingered down into the ridgeline spurs.
Each spur of ridgeline was a mighty finger.

### II.

High over this autumn world in blue-sky roof,
God's brilliant lamps blinked for me
While I stood on this summit
Looking over darkness in the valley.
This was a way to summarize the world
To see the dark outlay of that
Which had once been my familiar portion.
To analyze each large and infinitesimal part
To know the direction of my ascension,
Or my declension,
In the remaining time still left for me to spend.

III.

But what about my dream through slumber breaking
In soft bed, between clean sheets, soft pillow under head,
Of this great autumn giant-world's waking,
His stretching, yawning, wiping sleep from his eyes.
From my bed I arose, dressed in my best
As if I were going to appear before
Presidents, Queens, Kings, and other mighty of the earth.
Then, I walked out into the predawn hour alone.
In cool starlight I stepped briskly.
I was my old self again.
Hurrying over the brown leaf-colored autumn dirt road
Curving like a reluctant serpent
Winding through the tall spring grass,
Looking for a prey, a living delicacy,
To fill his long gaunt body's hunger.

IV.

For everywhere, the brown roads run in autumn
To join trunk lines of asphalt-gray,
Across the mountain, plain, valley, and bottom,
To feed cities' commerce night and day.
I followed the brown road up the valley
Where it dispersed among a dozen paths—
Fragmentary trails that led to nowhere.
I followed the knuckle roads,
On the big boney fingers higher, higher,
To be closer to the stars that blinked for me.

## V.

Darkness is never an obstacle of obstruction
Nor the bulwark of night when possessed with the inner
dreams
Waking in the autumn nighttime with a plan,
With the dream of seeing,
Where there is no other being
The secrets in the autumn earth's transitional schemes.

God's earth is so big and mightily solid
For my little steps, following where the brown road,
Color of autumn leaves, leads me.
Light as a wind-blown October leaf,
My steps upon the wrinkled skin of living earth,
My eyes up level with the stars,
I walked into the night.
My steps too light to tickle
Earth's wrinkled skin to make him laugh.

## VI.

Joyously, happily, my heart full of love I walked
To this high summit bringing with me
Only the invisible parts of life's dreams that count.
I brought love with me, understanding, tolerance,
The curiosity of one's going where something is about to hap-
pen.
I brought my happy heart
Wherein this beginning autumn of life,
With doors closed to greed, malice, intolerance, jealousy;
With doors from the earth to the stars

58

All opened wide for kindness, love and good will toward all
    men.
Night would never hold me back again.
In my surefooted, positive way,
I had climbed this high to be close to the stars.

    VII.

Only once had I stopped to hear
A pair of wild birds talking to each other in their night.
A brushpile by a dwindling little stream,
Was home to them back in the center
Safe from prowling fox.
I stood beside their kind of home
And listened to the love words of their language.
I felt their words but couldn't understand
Their deeper meaning
Where the dwindling stream mumbled in low tones
Words beautiful, sad, akin to poetry.
Akin to earth, to everything thereon.
Earth has the one gruff voice of thunder,
His many other voices are soft, musical, soothing and pleas-
    ant
For a giant so rugged, large and powerful.

    VIII.

Earth waking,
Early morning blowing the lamps of bright stars out,
Leaving the ceiling with bright indigo blue.
Earth coming alive,

While I, a living man, a kingdom within myself,
A living portion of earth's flesh,
A borrowed dirt
Looked on to dream, to think, to love, to capture
Everything within my sight,
To store without a reason except that one
Which makes a man a curious creature.

Beautiful dawn breaking,
Heavy eyelids of the mighty earth
Now going up to greet the light of day.

### IX.

This earth, a mighty living giant,
Cannot throw me off his back
For I am man.
I will have my say before the end
When he has hidden me,
If in my game of hide and seek with him,
Like a wild hare with the hounds,
I can dodge him long enough.
The little I have borrowed from him,
I shall return with interest.

### X.

So wonderful to see the giant world awake
From drowsy slumber,
Standing in the autumn-brown broomsedge up to my waist
Breathing a summit wind
Color and taste like Burgundy wine.

60

Now with the morning's welcoming
The sunball from the far east,
The earth has been awakened
And I have seen his secrets.
I have watched him rub the sleep from his eyes
From wrinkled skin
Up to the indigo blue morning skies.

With all the change within my heart
Within this kingdom of earth's living borrowed dust,
I shall descend from these heights for I must
Walk down the winding brown path to my valley,
Descend to depths so I will know when I am high
Enough to touch the stars
And to appreciate this height.

XI.

Descending to the valley
Now the earth's awake
Without a wink of sleep in bright-blue, softwind eyes.
My dream that woke me in the night,
That urge that drove me through the darkness
On a dimly starlit road
Has been fulfilled to satisfaction.
Transition of the earth
From summer unto autumn
With many changes
Has been transition in my heart
From darkness to the light,
From death unto the morning.

## XII.

Now clothed transitional earth,
Of which I am in living dust
An infinitesimal, borrowed part;
And of this, a fraction is my heart
Now big enough in its embrace
To reach the windows of the sky
Which are no higher than this heart is high.
I, who have struggled up the dark and rough terrain
Somewhere within its wilderness of paths I met
A traveler on all roads and at all times.
After I spoke to Death and shook his hand
He left me free with my new lease on life.
I vowed the second half would not be spent in vain.
Without conflicts of mankind within my heart
I stood upon the threshold in my zero hour
Wherein I witnessed a rebirth
When God's own light dissolved the darkness
In conflict for the final power.

# My heart tells me

My path shall be a trail of blowing wind
That leads me back to dark hills in the west;
I will arise and go to my own kin,
Back to my youthful dream of work and rest.
And if my path is long
                              I do not care!
And if my path is steep,
                              Then, I shall climb!
My heart tells me I must be going where
I shall remain contentedly this time.
For, as the wind is free, I shall be free!
The white mane of the wind shall be my guide
To hollows where whiteoaks root furtively,
To cone-shaped hills of home,
                              My love: my pride.
With heart aflame,
                    My voice will rise in song.
Westward, tonight!
                    Back to my lonely hollow!
My heart tells me that I am going strong,
That wind will be the path that I must follow.

# Come let us sing

Come everyone and let us sing together
While Scottish thistle fleece floats on the wind;
Come let us sing in bright October weather
Before the golden poplar tops have thinned!
Come let us sing before our blood grows cold,
This is the time because we feel we must;
The oak and sweet gum leaves have turned to gold,
We ought to sing a requiem for their dust.
It won't be long the powers of life remain
Before these husky hills bring back leaf blood.
Let's beat the singing wind and mournful rain
In our hilarious and exciting mood.
These days are passing now and we grow older,
Come, lift your voices high my faithful friends;
Come now, because our season has grown colder,
Come let us sing before our autumn ends!

# Unseasonable sinning

It's not the time for summer rain to fall
And stir the roots of grass.

                      This is December.

It's not the time for summer birds to call
Among the sumacs and the leafless timber.
It's not the time for flowers.

                      This is winter.

But everywhere rain is caressing grass.
The cress has shot up like a green oak splinter.
Green willow wands nod to us when we pass.
Our Mother Earth has been a steady thing,
Her seasons sometimes vary in beginnings,
Through summer, autumn, winter unto spring,
But these are not unseasonable sinnings.
Though summer rain from gray December skies
Is rare exception that cannot be good
For channels fill, streams leap, and rivers rise!
This is the real beginning of a flood!

# Soliloquy of the wild rose in the rock

An angry winter wind cast me up here—
A ripened autumn seed the wild rose bore;
Wind left me on this rock cold and severe,
Spring thaw found me beneath a muddy floor.
The hungry birds who searched for winter seeds,
Winged over with the winter wind's cold moan;
They found enough somewhere to fill their needs;
I found a crevice in this rugged stone.
The soft warm rains of spring soaked down to me,
Then downward from my seed went dark-hair roots
And I was born in this eternity
While suns of spring caressed my tiny shoots.
From this infertile crevice where I bloom
Young lovers found me with their eager eyes;
I go with them beyond my rockcliff room,
Let other wild flowers feed the butterflies!

# I have a path

I have a path that leads to my retreat—
A footpath undiscerning eyes will lose
But I can follow blindly with my feet
At any hour of darkest night I choose.
On starless, moonless nights I've found my way
Over rock ridges to my valley shack
And heard among dead leaves the foxes play
And cozy night birds twitter in grain stack.
I know my realm of valley is the place
Where fox and man can live the way they please,
Where winter wind will dry a sweaty face
And rustle whiteoak leaves still on the trees.
Each bend of path I have long memorized
In darkness, sunshine, sleet and rain and mud;
Never a step on it have I despised,
A lonely path is good to stir the mood.

# Boy or calf

How would you like to be a little calf
Who knows his mother for a time so brief,
Born and orphaned and a homeless waif
Between the birth of bud and fall of leaf?
Would you have fun among your cattle kind
To have an owner feed you scanty fare
Or plenty for a purpose? Would you mind
To live life's episode without a care?
How would it be after your breathing air
Fresh from the valley, mountain, western plain
On a crowded car to the cattle market where
You could not feed on sweet grass, feel the rain
And sleep on misty meadows under stars,
Never again to have dreams in your head
Of the world beyond your fence and pasture bars?
Now, would you rather be a boy instead
To have your world unfenced, to play and laugh
In life's great episode of fun and joy?
Have you ever heard of a laughing calf?
Have you ever known a bawling boy?

# Our heritage

We are a part of this rough land
Deep-rooted like the tree.
We've plowed this dirt with calloused hand
More than a century.

We know each cowbell's ringing here
Which tells the time of day.
We know the slopes to plant each year,
What our folks do and say.

We know the signals of each horn
And the messages they send
At set of sun or early morn
Upon a blowing wind.

When we lie down in bed at night
And hear a foxhorn blow,
We often rise, take lantern light,
Untie our hounds and go.

We like to follow hounds that chase
The fox until the morn
Then go back home with sleepy face
And on to plow the corn.

There is not one who does not love
A field and farming ground,
With sky and stars a roof above
And a companion hound!

We love this land we've always known
That holds us and our dead—
The rugged slopes with scattered stone
That grow our daily bread.

We love the lyric barking hound
And a piping horn that trills.
We love our high upheavaled ground,
Our heritage of hills.

# Free ride

When he implaned in Dallas
A pestering airways guest
To ride the constellation
I queried why this pest
Should be Chicago bound.

Whom did he plan to see?
Why he chose the skyway?
And why his ride was free?

Before the perfect landing
Our guest approached the door
Ignoring signs and manners
And those he rushed before.

Soon as the door was opened
And steps for us let down
This Texas fly was greeting
A fly whom he was meeting
In big Chicago town.

# The heart flies home

Though you are there tonight and I am here
You must not doubt my heart is flying home
To you when autumn leaves are brown and sere
And stars are bright as honey in the comb.
Designs of leaves are in the dress you wear
As you walk where the autumn leaves jump down
From tall treetops into your autumn hair.
The sere leaves fall until earth wears a gown.
After a walk you sit before the fire
Feeling the cheerful heat from oak and pine
Reading a book till midnight then retire
To a clean, cool bed in a home that's yours and mine.
If wheels will roll on rails of shining steel
And wings will climb up mountains of bright wind,
Soon I shall be with you where we can feel
The time is now and leave the past behind.

# April night and the singing winds

I choose this night and know the path to take
Through sumacs, red oaks, winding like a snake.

Night voices call me back where I belong,
To rising winds that sing a red-brush song.

The sickle moon hangs low above the hills
And beams upon the splashing April rills.

So many times to me old men have said
That April winds at night sing for the dead.

The dead tonight lie on the Plum Grove hill
Beneath new love songs of the whippoorwill.

I'll choose this night with winking stars and moon
That has gone down beyond the hills too soon.

I like the life on earth though it be brief,
And likened to the season of the leaf.

My blood goes up like warm sap in the tree,
I run on paths where foxes ought to be.

My blood runs wild but wilder is my mood;
I'm free to listen to the music flood!

Let wild winds sing across the April night
And dreamers ride the winds in gold starlight!

I'm glad to follow fox paths, shout and sing
I am alive on a night in April spring!

# Spring world, awake

Too late, Spring World, to sleep beneath a cover!
Wake now beneath your blanket of thin frost!
Pairs of nest-searching crows are flying over
And not for long can Winter be your host.
When soft lips of the roots are making sound
And sun is warming sap to stir again,
I'll put my ears against the fertile ground
To listen to sounds soothing as the rain.
So soon from virile dirt you will rise up
From this prolific earth to windy skies
And bring with you the long-stemmed buttercup
With multicolored wings of butterflies.
Who can believe the earth is still asleep
When your creators are down there astir
Fomenting their rebellion in the deep
To lift your world of beauty everywhere!

# Of dead leaves

Autumn has come—
Dead leaves are flying,
The wild birds call,
The corn is dying.

The kildees cry
Across the meadows,
The milkweed furze
Chase autumn shadows.

The corn is husked,
Husked corn comes in,
In yellow heaps
Into the bin.

Over the hills
The ghost-leaves fly—
Brown, scarlet, gold—
Toward the sky.

And it is good
The way I feel,
For I have corn
To grind in meal.

Let winter come
And life be dead,
And fields sleep white,
I have my bread.

I have my bread,
I have corn seed,
And that is all
I think I need.

And let lean shadows
Fall on the snow,
Lean tree shadows
In sunset glow.

Let rivers run
Blue through the snow,
Blue water in
The sunset glow.

Let pine trees whisper
To the bright wind
Of warm spring days
Soon to begin.

Let grass roots whisper
Of the season
When new life stirs
Without a reason.

One season past,
Another begins,
Time on and on
Like futile winds.

# House in the wind

Lean hungry wind goes out, fat wind comes in
And whistles like a lonesome violin.

The fox hounds sleep upon the windy hill;
The fox goes free to roam and prowl and kill.

A fox that wags his wet and slimy tail
And says the wind makes him a decent jail.

A wind that beats in rags a tin-pan tune!
A wind, low-down that loves a vulgar moon.

A wind that flirts with stuffed-in window rags
Quite sissy-like and struts and steals and brags.

The rat is right—must be the house's asleep;
This black box where the wall-plate vipers creep.

This rat he has some smarty things to say,
This prissy rat that long has had his way.

This rat, blue rat, with whiskers on his nose;
This silly rat that preens his scissor-toes.

A rat's a rat where-ever, ever he goes,
He writes a language no one reads or knows.

This rat is silly and this rat is not,
This rat lives in a rusty coffeepot.

The wind has kissed blue rat, for this I saw,
Blue rat then called the wind his mother-in-law.

A mountain cabin saw their honeymoon;
The rat is jealous since wind loves the moon.

Weeds choke the yards, the orchards ceased to bear,
And what of that—who'd pick the fruit or care?

No cider's made to jig the farm boys round;
The wine-saps lie and rot upon the ground.

Charlie drank cider from this orchard last;
Charlie and Nick and Jim all lived too fast.

Dead now and lost they are—the moon won't lie;
The moon's near heaven—see! the moon's up high!
Blue rat won't tell but knows just where they lie.

And Liz and Meg and Kate all full of lust
Are dead—now dead with lips a pinch of dust.

Like women old with black and thread-bare shawls,
This clapboard roof now leans and shrieks and sprawls.

This crazy wind blows in and it blows out!
It blows away somewhere—somewhere about.

Blows in rooms with walls thin as a rind;
Now in the wind a room is hard to find.

I loaf around with wind that loves my face;
We cannot find a room—not any place.

I hear a song of the long, long long-ago;
A corn-field voice is crooning, "Old Black Joe."

A sunny-voice—goodness, I'd like to know
"Old Uncle Ned," his fiddle and his bow.

The time is here the cabin's mossy bones
Are now a hidden heap of reddish stones.

Old reddish stones in deep-blue April grass
Where often snakes but people seldom pass.

Where shoe-string vines grow tall and growing run
To hide the lizards bathing in the sun.

Blue rat get out of here! Get out I say!
You and the wind too long have had your way.

You're married now—live happily together;
Measure your love with baskets of the weather.

I have come back to run this place awhile,
Blue rat now hide your alligator smile.

Blue rat I'll let you know I have come in,
I'll kick you hard enough to break your skin!

Get out of here! Forever let it be—
You rat with a long long pedigree!

You carefree rat that knows no thing of me,
You live where lives the mountain heart of me.

# An oak is oak

An oak can't be transplanted to a box,
Though fragile now, this sprig has tender shoots;
An oak belongs in loam among the rocks
With acorn husks attached to white-hair roots.
The oak will thrive on ledge and slope and bluff
Where its expanding roots are fed by loam.
A box can't feed one sustenance enough,
An oak can't drink the sunlight in your home.
Oak's roots can penetrate your floors to earth,
Its top can split your roof to reach the skies;
An oak is oak from the acorn of its birth;
An oak will be an oak until it dies.
Oak's roots can crumble rocks for sustenance,
The shapely leaves drink wind and sun and rain,
And sturdy arms can spread in grim defiance!
Take this plant back and leave it wild again!

# What is life worth?

My birds awaken me at break of dawn
By hungry chatter in the viney leaves,
And I arise and put a man's clothes on
Instead of robe and soft pajama sleeves.
I have returned to life I knew but lost
And, happily, I shall be with again.
Sounds, sights, and dreams I knew and loved the most
On small creek meadow and high hill terrain.
My world is small with oaks and pines and rocks
And wind in sedge and brier upon earth's floor,
The cawing crow, a distant barking fox
And singing, blue and clean the streams that pour
Down narrow channels in the bright moonlight
And pin the stars and moon down to the earth
I see before retiring for the night!
I'm proud that now I know what life is worth.

# World of springtimes past

Like moth wings in warm spring her dreams instead
Stir where the crocus blooms and wild birds sing,
And violets rise from their ancient bed
To feel and touch the pulse of poignant spring.
While she is in this world of springtimes past
She's not alone for a youthful man is there.
His coming tells her springtime love can last,
Though only she can see him young and fair.
With them are six who prattled at their knees
With cries and laughter that they liked to hear
In their old home beneath age-harried trees.
She sees her violets rise up each year
And crocuses flaunt blooms of windy gold
Where dream and spring will not let her grow old.

# Prolific dirt

By-product of prolific dirt am I,
Alive, ambitious, walk and talk and sing;
My mind can travel depths from earth to sky,
In winter I can see and write of spring.
The substance of prolific dirt is tree
Adjustable to climate and to clime;
This dirt can die, can live, has destiny,
Is nondestructible to passing time.
Prolific dirt is substance of the flower,
Its stem, bud, blossom, leaf and silken petal,
A loveliness that haunts us in its hour;
Prolific dirt, our dream, our fight, our metal!
Basis for beauty, life and all desire,
Retainer of the millions gone before,
Bulwark against the bomb, immune to fire,
Prolific dirt, eternal evermore!

# Spring song

This night we love as hand-in-hand we walk
A narrow path that leads us home too soon—
The cornblades sparkle in the clean-kept balk
And misty white clouds float across the moon.
This is the time for love—night in its splendor
Of dew-wet fields, corn, furrow, wind and star
And with sweet-williams' blossoms blue and tender
Beside the winding footpath where we are.
This valley stream we love is silvery white,
Its murmurs mock the whippoorwill's sad song;
Bright ribbon rippling in this soft moonlight
Will sing forever here where we belong.
Tonight we love as if this is our last
Because we witness spring and youth go past.

# Back where I belong

I thank God that he granted my stay here
To count the many songs in winds that blow.
When April spring returns again this year,
I'll walk with him where rivers rise and flow.
I'll stand beneath the gray-barked sycamore
And with soft hands I'll feel its scaly bark.
Not any man will ever love life more.
I'll pray as I walk in the April dark.
Death held me prisoner till God stepped in
And took me by the hand and gave me breath,
And I was glad this heart was cleansed of sin
And that I followed him from arms of death.
Back to my valley for the blooming spring,
Back to my garden and the wild bird's song,
To shadow, sun and multicolored wind,
The land, God must believe, where I belong.

# Hold April

Hold on to April; never let her pass!
Another year before she comes again
To bring us wind as clean as polished glass
And apple blossoms in soft, silver rain.
Hold April when there's music in the air,
When life is resurrected like a dream,
When wild birds sing up flights of windy stair
And bees love alder blossoms by the stream.
Hold April's face close yours and look afar,
Hold April in your arms in dear romance;
While holding her look to the sun and star
And with her in her faerie dreamland dance.
Do not let April go but hold her tight,
Month of eternal beauty and delight.

# Desolation

The farm's asleep, must be the house is too;
So lonesome here, sleep's all they both can do.

Smoke house is sunken, the barn is unkept;
Yard's dry as desert-bone and clean wind-swept,

The slow uncertain shadows cross the place;
White thunder clouds go drifting out to space.

The empty rooms are dark as ghostly sin;
The windows gone, the whistling winds drive in.

Some lanky cattle bawl and house dogs howl,
And for the backyard grapes slim foxes prowl.

The hungry rats from under floors have scrawled
Their names on doors and sills and stones high-walled.

A crow flaps down to gather straws and sticks
And caw-caws where—where are those country hicks?

The old cook stove is here all rusted red;
The wind laughs where the children cried for bread.

The hands that made the wines and killed the fleas,
Lie warm beneath this bank of chestnut trees.

Old Buck who drank the strong rebellious wine
Sleeps by his Kate where bramble briers entwine.

His young son Buck who took a risky chance
Smashed in a plane three miles from Verdun, France.

And George and Frank both fond of gun and gin
Now sleep in earth with what they fought to win.

They got all heady spiked on homemade wines
And tried to end the war in German lines.

Charlie was brought back from a drunken brawl;
He pulled his gun too late and that was all.

And Meg went out one day to fix the fence;
She and Jake Hix were never heard of since.

And Liz and Kate and Will went West in haste;
They wanted something new to suit their taste.

They got it, for they never have been back
To see old friends and drink the apple-jack.

They don't return; they're too, too far away;
Maybe they dream they'll rise again someday.

Maybe to return to where their kin have lain
Beneath the tom-tom thrums of windless rain.

A flag floats high above each tall son's grave,
Not for his actual worth but what he gave.

The rest have boards to tell their worldly deeds;
That's less conceit and all a person needs.

# My love must learn

I hate to tear it down with my own hands,
I'd rather leave it for the birds and mice;
But I must act since present Time commands,
My young wife wants a home that's new and nice.
I must be brave and tear it to the ground,
Rip clapboards and disperse the chimney rocks
So wind can whistle with a throaty sound
Where it once stood, through rose and hollyhocks.
My young wife says, down with this ancient house,
And she demands that where it stood must rise
A smaller house immune to wind and mouse,
A modern structure soothing to the eyes.
But I'll be watching for them to return,
The generations who have gone will care;
Though my young wife demands, she soon will learn
Where she hears knocking and finds no one there.

# Voices of spring

To see a winter world reborn to this,
Sunshine and shadow and the voice of spring,
To be alive and part of springtime bliss,
To hear leaves rustle and the wild birds sing,
Make this our greatest season to rejoice.
From harried winter's cold cocoon has come
A world that sings in one united voice
With balmy winds in leaves and bees' loud hum
In clouds of dogwood blossoms on the slopes.
Enchanted time when blooms reach for the sky
And fill us with invigorating hopes,
We cannot understand why all must die,
Why spring most beautiful must soonest pass
And leave its white rain on enduring grass.

# The ballad of the bride

*My bride don't like the mountain shack,*
*She wants a house of stone;*
*My Love has said she's going back*
*To life that is her own.*
*What shall I do for I can't lose*
*My bride in gowns so fine,*
*Who walks in fifty dollar shoes*
*And loves her cakes and wine!*

A bride can strut in gowns so fine
And fifty dollar shoes;
A mountain man should always mind
The kind of bride to choose.
And you can have your big fine house
And we will keep the shack,
And when you get your city house
Your heart will turn you back!

*Your ways are dark and I shall take*
*My bride unto the town*
*Where lonesome mountain winds can't break*
*The heart beneath her gown.*
*I'll take her to the shining streets*
*Away from paths of mud*

*Where people wear good clothes, she greets*
*Among her people's blood.*


The mountain blood in a mountain man
Sired where these waters run,
Is always blood of a mountain man
And thicker blood, my Son.
The mountain blood in a mountain girl
Is your own kind, my Son;
It'll stand by you when your fine world
Has quickly come undone.


*I do not care for a mountain lass*
*Who cannot wear her clothes;*
*My Love, dear Mother, must have class*
*In any place she goes.*
*Her dainty lips must sip the wine,*
*Her swan-white bosom show,*
*And on her fingers diamonds shine*
*Like patches of the snow.*


Your bride can drink the costly wine
And eat the sweetest cake,
And she can leave your oak and pine
And sounds your lone winds make.
And she can wear her diamond ring
That glistens like the snow,
And she can be the dainty thing
With snow-white breasts to show.

Remember Son, that mountain blood
Is very slow to change,
And you will long for paths of mud
And mountains for a change.
You'll long to hear your old fox horn,
The crack of your shot-gun.
You'll long to plow the newground corn
And hear these waters run.

And you can have your big fine house
But we will keep the shack,
And when you get the big stone house
You'll want the old logs back.
Your father sired you in a shack
Where lonesome waters run,
With the world's best cloth upon your back
You will return, my Son.


II


*Mother, I've been two years away*
*In a mansion made of stone.*
*I left my Love and ran away*
*Back to these things I own.*
*I could not buy her costly wine*
*Nor fifty dollar shoes,*
*Nor diamonds like the stars that shine*
*And gowns my Love would choose.*
*I want to hear the hunter's horn,*
*I want to shoot my gun,*

*I want to smell the growing corn*
*And hear the waters run.*
*I do not want the house of stone,*
*I only want the shack,*
*To eat the food that is my own*
*And have my old bed back.*

*I want to sickle slopes of grain*
*And walk on paths of mud,*
*I want to live my life again*
*And be my father's blood.*
*My second bride a mountain girl,*
*My first True Love will be,*
*Then I can sing and I can shout*
*The world belongs to me!*

# Ides of March

The new-leafed birch beside the river dreams;
May apples spring from loam on tender stems.

Lean, hungry cattle prowl on greening hill
Searching for bullgrass and the daffodil.

The sun has thawed the winter's sleeping snake,
And one might be on any path you take.

Before the white-oak blossoms burst in full
Sheep have grown restless in their winter wool.

The cows steal out to calve in alder brush
Always so near a nest of singing thrush.

But slopes are filled with poke and turnip greens.
Potatoes gone and leather britches beans.

Potatoes pop up through the loamy mould
And sawbriers strut their leaves of windy gold.

Go to the yard and chase away the ox,
He's broken through to get the hollyhocks.

It's time the cattle should have exercise,
March wind is soothing to their winter eyes.

Foxes connive to show the hounds some speed,
Chickens to catch and little mouths to feed.

Welcome just anytime, conniving fox,
Five hound dogs snore behind the stovewood box.

How pleasant is the sun in heaven's arch
But earth is restless on the Ides of March.

# One body

One body I have driven furiously,
A stalwart body through its youth and prime,
So much to do,
                so many things to see,
I drove it on,
                until there came a time.
Clay body built
                for labor, dream, and strife.
Kingdom of God,
                man should hold in esteem—
Body and spirit are together life,
Body and spirit are together dream.
Unmerciful,
                I forced it to accept
Food to stale blood,
                poisons to paralyze;
Protective rules
                were things I never kept
For tired brain,
                life-giving heart and eyes.
This body I have driven is my own,
My only one to serve me to the end;
With things to do and see and good years flown,
I'll slow at last to treat it like a friend.

# Their eyes have seen

He sees them walking slowly by the stream
Their small hands holding book and dinner pail,
They are awake to life and do not dream,
They shout to wind and mock the calling quail
With laughter ringing through the thin blue air
As boys run for the old persimmon grove
To pick up mellowed fruit frost-ripened there
To share with little rose-lipped girls they love.
This wakes the old man's dreams and memories
Of life that goes back fifty years and more
When coming home from school he pillaged these
Wild groves for the lady by him in the door
Whose hair, like his, is white as moonlit snow.
Each morn and afternoon they watch them pass,
Remembering youth carefree as winds that blow
And steps once light as raindrops on the grass.

# Old Christmas

When I walked out across the snow
I heard the cattle low and low.

And there they stood around the barn,
Pawing the snow to keep them warm.

These long-haired cattle in the glow
Of yellow sun and bluejohn snow.

Murt says to me: "Alf, there's the moon,
You'd better feed the cattle soon."

"So strange but there's the moon," says I,
"The moon and sun both in the sky.

"Though it is early for the moon,
I'll go and feed the cattle soon."

The sun went down behind a cloud;
The frosty wind blew cold and loud.

The sun went down, the barn was lost;
The earth looked like a graveyard ghost.

And I went back, went in a hurry;
Was blinded by the big snow flurry.

Says I: "Murt, you're contrary!"
Says she: "It's sixth of January!

"This day Lord Jesus first saw light,
Was not on no December night.

"Folks got it wrong—this was the day—
Alf, have you fed the milk cows hay?"

We listen'd to the yearlings low;
We listen'd to the roosters crow.

Murt says: "That proves it is a fact
Way chickens and the cattle act!

"It was the sixth of January
That's why we have this big snow flurry."

Yes wind is wind, a fact's a fact;
I put the rag back in the crack.

'Pears like it chilled my blood, the wind;
That wind that kept a-coming in.

And Murt she says: "The alders leaf,
Because it's Christ's birthday they leaf.

"My mother's mother said she knew
That, that was why the alders grew

"Nothing like that in old December.
Now just think back, do you remember?"

When this was over I went out
And stretched my arms and stirred about.

I fed the milk cows forks of hay
To calm them in a sort of way.

I called the chickens to the crib
And shelled them corn to stop their gib.

And when I went to feed the pigs
I found the leafed out alder twigs.

So green and pretty in the snow
After the storm in sunset glow.

I had to stop and shed some tears
The way folks slander Christ these years.

# Small wonder

America, when I was born I found you,
And when I sang, you grew into my song;
With all your friendliness and warmth around you
You made my singing joyful, loud and strong.
Your rugged hilltop was my place of birth,
Your Sandy River mine since life began;
The upland acres of your fruitful earth
I plowed and hoed before I was a man.
Your strength is in my heart, my brain, my blood,
Your water, wind and soil have nourished me,
Your seasons' winds have put in me a mood,
Your wild hawks' freedom taught me to be free.
I'm product-of and moulded from your clay,
Prolific earth of which I am a part.
My nights are nothingness, short is my day,
Small wonder your songs grow within my heart.

# Light and shadow

Invisible hands are now dispersing dew
On morning-glory bell and buttercup—
Long, unseen arms extend across wind-blue
To gather all the jewel dewdrops up.
The spiders' silver strands in homes respun
From seeded crabgrass stem to bullgrass blade,
Must give their decorations to the sun,
Return the gifts that silent night has made.
And unseen fingers on these hands have found
The baby-handed moles that love the night
And sent them back to holes deep underground.
Moles' little eyes were not made for the light.
Invisible hands of light have found their own,
Dewdrop and mole and silver strand and flower,
Dispersed of all the darkness night has sown—
Light over darkness has a final power.

# Be in a joyful mood

Be in a joyful mood and walk with me
Into beginning Spring's cool solitudes
Where streamlets sing so inconsistently
And singing birds are busy in the woods.
All nature now begins to harmonize
Since percoon eases through the deadleaf mold
To flaunt white banners to the windblue skies
In young, strong winds of spring still winter-cold.
The highest mind today is not enough
To celebrate the long-awaited Spring
And greet the snowy percoon on the bluff
And watch song sparrows rise and hear them sing.
Our spirits must be high to go and find
Nature's perfection in the flower and tree
And solitude that will inspire the mind
When we are part of all this harmony.

# Two leaves

The multicolored hosts drift down the sky,
Hand-heart-star-shaped and autumn-light and thin,
And you and I are two leaves drifting by
With other loves in legions of the wind.
Look up, my love, don't turn your head away,
Look high, my love, as if you were a star;
You are the golden leaf, I am the gray
And we go drifting as the others are.
Come, put your hand in mine, let's not pretend,
For love is just as high as we are high.
We'll travel on the silver lanes of wind
Among the other lovers in the sky.

# Empty house

This is the empty house I hate to pass
For I have watched it sagging to decay;
Each year more briers move in to choke the grass
Since they have taken my playmates away.
The rotting shingle roof now needs repairs
For boards have curled like sawbriers in the sun;
Now, no one ever stops here. No one cares
To walk paths where Virginia creepers run,
To step near broken glass from window panes.
Sumacs and tall horseweeds are growing now
Where only part of their old barn remains,
Enough to hide their rusty disk and plow.
Here once we played in hollyhock and fern,
Beneath loud bees on springtime's snowy hair;
When they moved out they said they would return,
Each day I go to see if they are there.

# For Martha Hylton Stuart

Soft, velvet grass erases all the scar
Where she now lies embedded for the night,
Beneath the sun, the ambient wind and star—
Amid the grass, her yuccas blossom white.
Her eyes have seen before these in their season
But cannot see them blossom now for her;
The quilt that she lies under is the reason,
So close where they and winds of April stir.
Hands that once plucked the yuccas for bouquets,
Each day, the vase refilled in every room,
Cannot reach through the walls of Plum Grove clay,
To touch again and fondle yucca bloom,
Nor can their dark-hair roots reach to her bed.
She and her flowers must remain apart,
Her living yuccas and the wreaths we spread,
Garlands of beauty too far from her heart.

Jesse Stuart is the well-known and well-loved poet, novelist, short-story writer, and author of *Man with a Bull-Tongue Plow, Taps for Private Tussie* (a Book-of-the-Month Club selection), *The Thread That Runs So True, Hie to the Hunters, The Year of My Rebirth, Plowshare in Heaven,* and many others. Mr. Stuart is a Kentuckian by birth, though he has traveled the world, and he is a teacher as well as a writer. His work has appeared in magazines throughout the country. He is also the author of four outstanding children's books—stories that have introduced a new generation of readers to Jesse Stuart's Kentucky hill people.

# ACKNOWLEDGMENTS

112

113